BATTLES
OF THE
AMERICAN
REVOLUTION

by Michael Burgan

Table of Contents

A Difficult Winter

The Revolution Begins

What sparked the first battle of the American Revolution, and how did the colonists fare in the first year of the war?

Wins and Losses

What were the major American victories and defeats through 1777?

War at Sea

What was the nature of naval warfare during the American Revolution?

The Road to Final Victory

How did the Americans manage to turn the tide against the British and win their independence?

4

6

16

28

30

36

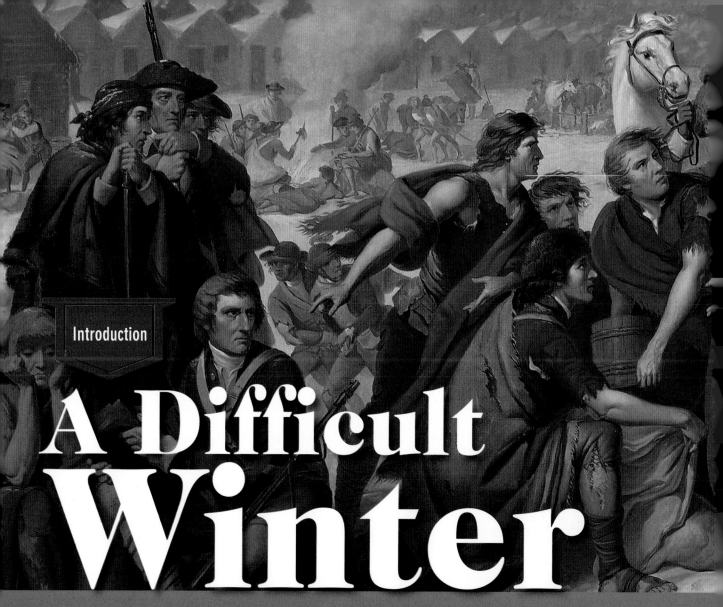

A Difficult Winter

It was 1777, before Christmas. In Valley Forge, Pennsylvania, thousands of American soldiers cut down trees to build small log cabins. Snow covered the ground. The men had fought the British throughout the spring, summer, and fall in New Jersey and Pennsylvania. Now both sides would rest for the winter. The soldiers would fight again in the spring.

Men from all thirteen British colonies were in the American army. The colonies had declared independence from Great Britain in July 1776. Most of the soldiers had family roots in Great Britain. Some soldiers came from other European nations. African Americans and Native Americans were also part of the army. The wives of some of the soldiers were with the army. The wives followed the troops, cooking and sewing for the men.

General George Washington led the American army. Congress had named Washington commander in chief of the Continental Army in June 1775, soon after the American Revolution began.

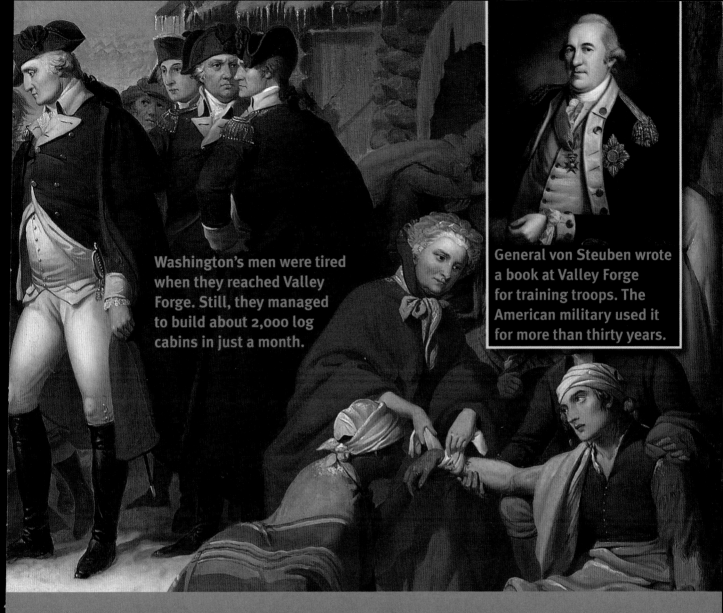

Washington's men were tired when they reached Valley Forge. Still, they managed to build about 2,000 log cabins in just a month.

General von Steuben wrote a book at Valley Forge for training troops. The American military used it for more than thirty years.

By 1777, George Washington and his men had won several key battles. But the Continental Army had lost other battles.

During the winter, Washington worried about the men. Often the soldiers did not have enough food. The men also did not have enough clothing and blankets. About 2,000 men died from the cold and illness. With all the troubles, Washington was able to keep the army together at Valley Forge.

A German officer, Friedrich Wilhelm Augustus von Steuben, arrived in February 1778. Von Steuben taught the American officers a better way to train the men. Von Steuben also explained the need for officers to show concern for the common soldier. The attention would make the troops more loyal. The troops would fight harder.

Why were the Americans fighting for independence? How would the army do on the battlefield in the future? Keep reading to learn about the key battles of the American Revolution.

The Revolution Begins

What sparked the first battle
of the American Revolution,
and how did the colonists
fare in the first year of the war?

Boston residents often called the British soldiers "Redcoats" or "Lobsterbacks," referring to the red jackets they wore.

Protests against the British took place in the city of Boston, Massachusetts. Starting in 1764, the British had angered many Americans. King George III and **Parliament** (PAR-lih-ment) (the British governing body) taxed the colonies. One tax was to help defend the **frontier** (frun-TEER), or land at the edge of the settlements. In 1775, British troops camped in Boston. The troops fought against **Patriots** (PAY-tree-uts)—the people who challenged British rule. People who supported Great Britain were called **Loyalists** (LOY-uh-lists).

HISTORICAL PERSPECTIVE

Taxes and Representation

For many Americans of the 1760s a key issue was taxation without representation. Both Americans and the British believed that taxes were fair only if they were imposed by elected officials who could voice the views of those citizens who elected them. But American colonists did not have representatives in Parliament that placed the new taxes on the colonies. This meant the colonies had no chance to speak out in Parliament against the taxes, which they considered unfair. British lawmakers replied that the Americans had "virtual representation," meaning that Parliament looked at the views of all citizens, whether they had representation or not and whether they lived in England or America. The lawmakers then did what was best for the nation. The Americans rejected this idea.

Growing Problems

In March 1770, an angry Boston crowd attacked a British soldier. Then, British soldiers killed five Americans. The event, called the Boston Massacre, made Patriots angry. Later, some Patriots threw British tea into the Boston Harbor. The "tea party" was a way to protest a tax on tea.

As punishment, Parliament passed a law to close Boston Harbor. British General Thomas Gage became the governor of Massachusetts.

Samuel Adams was a Patriot leader in Boston. Adams asked people to stop buying and selling British goods. A **boycott** (BOY-kaht) is the word used today to describe such an action. Some Patriots wanted representatives in a new Continental Congress to talk about what to do. Meanwhile, men in towns of Massachusetts formed an army called a **militia** (mih-LIH-shuh). The militia trained to fight the British.

▲ Paul Revere created this poster about the Boston Massacre. He won greater fame in 1775 when he warned other Patriots that British troops were marching out of Boston to confiscate colonial arms in nearby Concord.

The Root of the Meaning

The word **casualty** comes from the Latin word *casualis*, which means "by chance, or by accident." In the late fifteenth century, casualty came to refer to "losses in number from a military troop."

A poem written during the nineteenth century described Paul Revere's "midnight ride" to warn that the British were coming.

The Fighting Begins

On the evening of April 18, 1775, about 700 British troops left Boston. The plan was to take weapons the colonists had stored in the town of Concord. Some Americans feared the British also planned to arrest two Patriot leaders, Samuel Adams and John Hancock. The two men were nearby in Lexington.

Paul Revere also left the city. Revere and two other Patriots rode out on horseback to spread the word that the British were coming.

By morning, militia troops, called **minutemen** (MIH-nut-men), were waiting in Lexington. As the British approached, someone fired a shot. No one knows who fired, but soon both sides were shooting. The British soldiers carried long-barreled guns called **muskets** (MUS-kets). At the end of the muskets were spears called **bayonets** (BAY-uh-nets). Eight Americans died and others were dying or wounded. The American Revolution had begun.

On to Concord

The British soldiers, called Redcoats, marched to Concord. Some Redcoats searched for Patriot weapons. Other Redcoats went to guard a bridge. At the bridge, Patriots attacked the British. Fighting was fierce as the British tried to **retreat** (rih-TREET), or turn back. American militia hid in houses, and behind trees and fences. The Patriots fired on the Redcoats. As the British soldiers headed back to Boston, more Patriots began shooting.

PRIMARY SOURCE

A British officer described the fighting during the retreat to Boston:

"Before we had gone a mile we were fired on from all sides, but mostly from the rear, where people had hid themselves in houses till we had passed, and then fired.... They were so concealed there was hardly any seeing them: in this way we marched between 9 and 10 miles, their numbers increasing from all parts, while ours was reducing by deaths, wounds, and fatigue ..."

▲ With more militia constantly arriving, the Americans greatly outnumbered the British by day's end.

A Deadly Day

A major battle took place at Menotomy. Today, the town is named Arlington, Massachusetts. The British burned some homes, trying to force out hiding shooters. Meanwhile, minutemen poured in from nearby. At the end of the battle, twenty-five Americans were dead.

In the battles and the British retreat to Boston, more British soldiers were killed than Americans. Over 200 British were wounded and 73 men were killed. The Americans lost about 50 men. The battle showed the British that the Patriots were ready to fight.

Early Victories

News of the fighting in Massachusetts spread throughout the colonies. In May, a Patriot named Ethan Allen led a group of men from Vermont toward Fort Ticonderoga, New York. Allen met up with another Patriot officer named Benedict Arnold. Together, the Patriots surprised the British and captured the fort, which had many large cannons. Now the Americans could use the large cannons against the British.

✔
CHECKPOINT
Talk About It

Colonists from across New England raced to help the rebels in Massachusetts. Discuss with a partner what cause or collective effort would make you leave your home to help others in need.

"Don't fire until I tell you! Don't fire till you see the whites of their eyes!"

Bunker Hill and Breed's Hill

In Massachusetts, thousands of American soldiers camped outside of Boston. The British still controlled the city, but General Gage wanted to take control of the nearby hills. The Americans learned of the plan and rushed to a place across the river from Boston, called Breed's Hill. The Americans built fences and a temporary structure used for defense, called a **redoubt** (rih-DAUT). The Patriots wanted protection from a British advance. But on June 17, 1775, the British fired on the American positions. The important battle that followed was named for a nearby high spot called Bunker Hill. Most historians still refer to the event as the Battle of Bunker Hill.

British canon fire weakened the American **line** (LINE)—the arrangement of soldiers. A famous story says that Colonel William Prescott told American soldiers before the battle: "Don't fire until I tell you! Don't fire till you see the whites of their eyes!" By following the order, the hope was for the meager amount of American supplies to be saved for as long as possible.

The British began sending more troops to the battle and attacked three times. The first two times, the Patriots waited patiently for the British to get close. Then the Americans fired several deadly rounds of ammunition.

On their third charge, the British finally entered the redoubt. Some Americans fought and died on Breed's Hill, while other Americans retreated.

Possibly, the British won the Battle of Bunker Hill because the Americans were forced off the high ground. More than 100 Patriots died. But the British paid a high price. More than 1,000 Redcoats were dead or wounded. Most important, the Patriots believed American troops could win against one of the greatest armies in the world.

PERSONAL PERSPECTIVE

American soldier John Chester described some of what he saw at Bunker Hill in a letter to a friend:

"We were in imminent [close] danger from the cannon-shot, which buzzed around us like hail."

Leaving Boston

George Washington arrived outside Boston. Washington had come to take over the soldiers of the Continental Army. The Continental Army continued to surround Boston and keep supplies away from the British, in an action called a **siege** (SEEJ).

Early in 1776, the cannons from Fort Ticonderoga arrived in Boston. Washington placed the cannons in the sight of the British. Because of the cannons, the British did not attack. Instead, the British left Boston in ships. Washington chose not to fight in order to keep the city from being destroyed. Soon, ships with many British soldiers arrived in New York.

THEY MADE A DIFFERENCE

Henry Knox (1750–1806)

Soon after the American Revolution began, George Washington put young Henry Knox in charge of the American artillery. Knox had the job of moving the guns from Fort Ticonderoga to Boston. He organized the hauling of some 60 tons of cannons over snow and frozen water. Knox became a trusted aide and friend to Washington and later served as the first head of the U.S. Department of War.

▲ Knox and his men used sleds to move cannons and supplies 485 kilometers (300 miles) from Fort Ticonderoga to Boston. The journey took 56 days.

Fighting in New York

The Continental Army was small and untrained compared with the British forces. In July 1776 the British reached Staten Island, New York. The main **campaign** (kam-PANE), or military operations, began. The British campaign challenged the Americans.

The First Battle

The British attacked American forces on Long Island, New York, on August 27, 1776. General William Howe, the British commander, managed to surprise the American forces. The Americans suffered great losses.

General Howe assumed that a British offer for peace would be accepted. American leaders rejected the offer but talks continued. Meanwhile, Washington worked out an American strategy for the rest of the war. The Continental Army would not start major battles. Instead, the Continental Army would fight only when attacked. Washington wanted to protect land controlled by Americans. Washington also wanted to wear down the British Army over time.

In this detailed plan, the positions of the British and American armies in New York are outlined. ▶

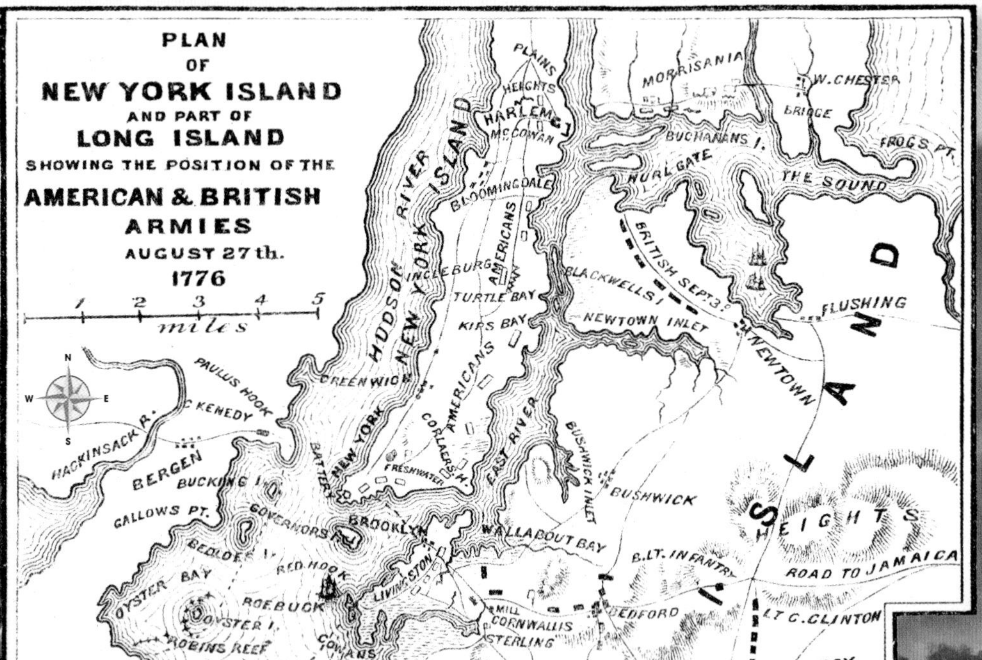

PLAN
OF
NEW YORK ISLAND
AND PART OF
LONG ISLAND
SHOWING THE POSITION OF THE
AMERICAN & BRITISH
ARMIES
AUGUST 27th.
1776

▲Loyalists on Long Island helped the British take a shortcut that allowed them to surprise the Americans.

The Americans Lose Manhattan

In September, the British attacked American troops stationed on the island of Manhattan. The British took the southern part of the island. Washington retreated to the north. At Harlem Heights, the Americans defeated an advancing British force. The Americans left one small force at Fort Washington in northern Manhattan. Other Americans remained across the river at Fort Lee, New Jersey. The main army of Washington then headed north above the island of Manhattan. On October 28, in White Plains, the two armies met. The British won a victory. But once again Washington was able to retreat.

Final Losses

Instead of chasing the Americans, Howe returned south. In November, the British stormed Fort Washington in Manhattan. To save thousands of American lives, the American officer in charge surrendered. Soon the British captured Fort Lee as well. Now the British had firm control of New York City.

"I only regret that I have but one life to give for my country."

▲ Nathan Hale, a soldier of Connecticut, is reported to have uttered these famous words before being hung as a spy: "I only regret that I have but one life to give for my country."

Summing Up

- Americans known as Patriots protested British laws that placed new taxes on the colonies. The protests were strongest in Boston, so Great Britain sent troops there.

- In April 1775, fighting broke out between the British and Massachusetts's militia in the towns of Lexington and Concord. The American Revolution was ignited.

- The next major battle, known as the Battle of Bunker Hill, took place at Breed's Hill just outside of Boston. In March 1776, George Washington forced the British to leave Boston. Both armies then headed to New York, where the first major campaign took place. The British surprised American troops on Long Island and then took control of Manhattan. By November, Washington had left New York.

Putting It All Together

Choose one of the following research activities. Work independently, in pairs, or in small groups. Share your responses with your class, and listen to others present their work.

1 Who were the Patriots that fought in the early battles of the American Revolution? Write a short paragraph describing who they were, how they learned to fight, and what they were fighting for. Who were the Loyalists? Write a short paragraph about who they were and some of the reasons why they remained loyal to Great Britain.

2 Draw a detailed map, or make a three-dimensional model or diorama, that illustrates one of the battles discussed in this chapter. Be sure to show the positions of the British and American forces.

3 In March 1775, Patriot Patrick Henry gave his famous speech in Virginia where he stated, "I know not what course others may take; but as for me, give me liberty or give me death!" Did his famous statement reflect Southern views at the time of the Revolution? Research to find out and use text evidence from multiple sources to support your answer.

Wins
and Losses

What were the major American victories and defeats through 1777?

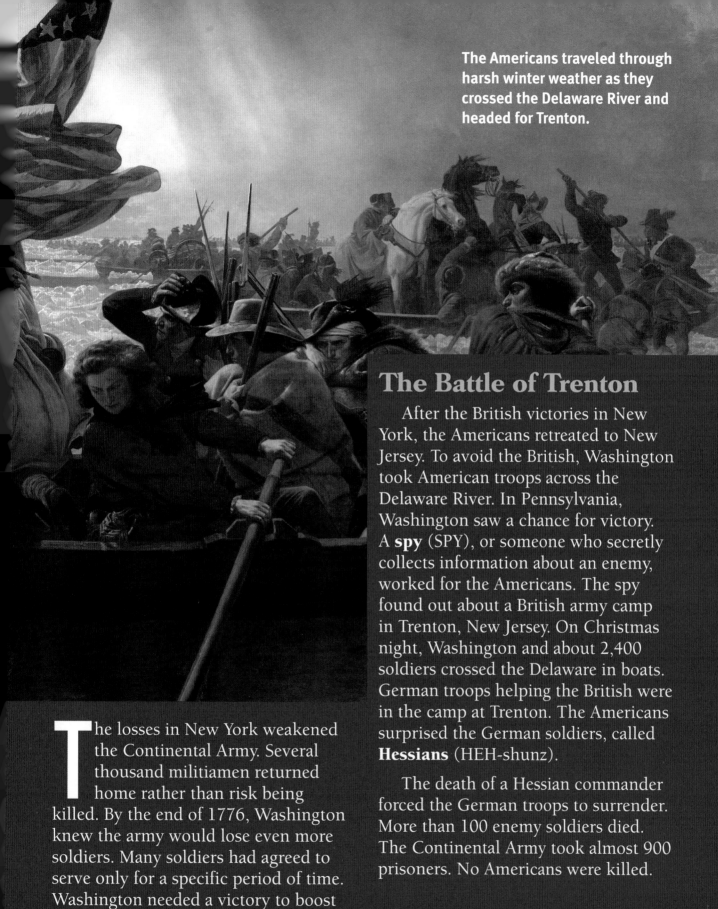

The Americans traveled through harsh winter weather as they crossed the Delaware River and headed for Trenton.

The Battle of Trenton

After the British victories in New York, the Americans retreated to New Jersey. To avoid the British, Washington took American troops across the Delaware River. In Pennsylvania, Washington saw a chance for victory. A **spy** (SPY), or someone who secretly collects information about an enemy, worked for the Americans. The spy found out about a British army camp in Trenton, New Jersey. On Christmas night, Washington and about 2,400 soldiers crossed the Delaware in boats. German troops helping the British were in the camp at Trenton. The Americans surprised the German soldiers, called **Hessians** (HEH-shunz).

The death of a Hessian commander forced the German troops to surrender. More than 100 enemy soldiers died. The Continental Army took almost 900 prisoners. No Americans were killed.

The losses in New York weakened the Continental Army. Several thousand militiamen returned home rather than risk being killed. By the end of 1776, Washington knew the army would lose even more soldiers. Many soldiers had agreed to serve only for a specific period of time. Washington needed a victory to boost the spirits of the army.

PRIMARY SOURCE

The American Crisis

Thomas Paine came from England to America in 1774. In December 1776, he wrote the first of thirteen articles called *The American Crisis* to boost the spirits of the soldiers and other Patriots. Here is part of that first article.

"These are the times that try men's souls. The summer soldier and the sunshine patriot will, in this crisis, shrink from the service of their country; but he that stands by it now, deserves the love and thanks of man and woman."

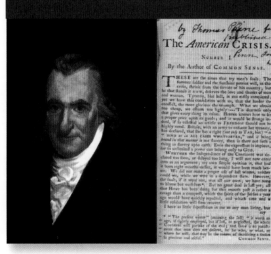

The Battle of Princeton

Next, Washington tricked the British. American troops were told to burn fires at night in camp. Some soldiers kept the fires burning so the camp looked full of people. But most of the soldiers attacked the British forces at Princeton, New Jersey. The Americans won a quick victory. The wins in New Jersey boosted the spirits of the Continental Army.

Losses in Pennsylvania

After Princeton, both armies camped until May 1777. When the fighting began again, General Howe moved British troops toward Philadelphia, the capital at the time. In June, the two armies fought in New Jersey. Then Howe moved British troops back to Staten Island in New York. From Staten Island, the British sailed into Chesapeake Bay and landed south of Philadelphia. On August 28, the British began to march to the city.

HISTORICAL PERSPECTIVE

Valley Forge

The food shortages at Valley Forge are well known. But the soldiers did not go hungry because there was no food in the area. Farmers had produced a good crop that fall. Many of them, however, preferred to sell to the British rather than to their own government. The British could pay in gold, while the Americans used paper money that had little value. Farmers could not buy what they needed to live with the American paper money. Moreover, some of them were Loyalists who opposed the war. They felt no duty to help the Patriots.

Brandywine

Meanwhile, Washington's army headed for Pennsylvania. In September, Washington positioned about 11,000 men along Brandywine Creek. Then the Americans waited for the British. Howe sent part of the British force toward the main American line and other soldiers to attack the Americans from behind. The army of Washington was fooled. The British forced an American retreat.

The British tried to force another major battle, but Washington avoided the fight. Howe took over Philadelphia. Howe left some troops in the city and sent other troops to Germantown.

Germantown

Washington decided to attack the divided British army. On October 4, 1777, the Americans met the British in Germantown. The fighting began well for the Americans. Then some British soldiers took over a stone house to use as a fort. Washington had a plan. But it was hard to carry out because of heavy gunfire and dense fog. The Americans lost the Battle of Germantown, but had come close to victory.

By December, the British were firmly in control of Philadelphia. Washington then set up winter camp at Valley Forge and planned for another year of battle.

▼ Because of the smoke from guns and the fog, some Americans fired at each other during the fighting at Germantown, something that happens in all wars.

▼ In Pennsylvania, the British promised to give Loyalists land and money if they signed up to fight the Patriots.

TEUCRO DUCE NIL DESPERANDOM.

First Battalion of PENNSYLVANIA LOYALISTS, commanded by His Excellency Sir WILLIAM HOWE, K B.

ALL INTREPID ABLE-BODIED

HEROES,

WHO are willing to serve His MAJESTY KING GEORGE the Third, in Defence of their Country, Laws and Constitution, against the arbitrary Usurpations of a tyrannical Congress, have now not only an Opportunity of manifesting their Spirit, by assisting in reducing to Obedience their too-long deluded Countrymen, but also of acquiring the polite Accomplishments of a Soldier, by serving only two Years, or during the present Rebellion in America.

Such spirited Fellows, who are willing to engage, will be rewarded at the End of the War, besides their Laurels, with 50 Acres of Land, where every gallant Hero may retire. . . . .

Each Volunteer will receive, as a Bounty, FIVE DOLLARS, besides Arms, Cloathing and Accoutrements, and every other Requisite proper to accommodate a Gentleman Soldier, by applying to Lieutenant Colonel ALLEN, or at Captain KEARNY's Rendezvous, at PATRICK TONRY's, three Doors above Market-street, in Second-street.

✔ CHECKPOINT

Reread

Reread the sections that describe how George Washington prepared for battles. What did he do to gain an advantage for his troops?

Away from Washington's Army

Not all the major battles of 1777 involved soldiers under Washington. American troops were in New England and northern New York State. The British hoped to cut off those parts of the country from the other states.

Danbury

In April 1777, British troops marched toward Danbury, Connecticut. Barns and warehouses in Danbury stored supplies for the Patriots. American troops could not stop the British from destroying many of the buildings. When leaving Danbury, the British met about 600 American soldiers. Benedict Arnold led the Americans in two days of fighting. A Loyalist helped the British escape to ships on the Long Island Sound.

Bennington

Starting in June, General John Burgoyne led British troops south from Canada into New York. A smaller British force in the west moved east through New York. A third British force planned to head north from New York City to Saratoga. The British planned to have the three forces meet and attack the Americans. Fortunately for the Americans, the plan failed.

▲ Sybil Ludington has been called the "female Paul Revere" for warning Connecticut militia the British were heading for Danbury when she was only sixteen years old.

The British troops arrived at Fort Ticonderoga on July 1. Burgoyne placed **artillery** (ar-TIH-ler-ee)—large guns usually moved on wheels— on a nearby mountain. The Americans gave up the fort rather than lose a battle.

In August, Burgoyne sent several hundred troops into Vermont. Local militia met the British outside of Bennington. The two sides fought for two hours. In the end, the Americans forced the British to flee. British **reinforcements** (ree-in-FORS-ments)— additional troops— arrived. But the Americans defeated the reinforcements. The loss for Burgoyne of lives and supplies was large and painful.

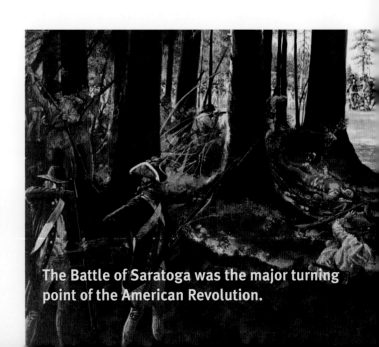

The Battle of Saratoga was the major turning point of the American Revolution.

Saratoga

Patriots welcomed the victory at Bennington. But Americans won an even more important battle at Saratoga. General Burgoyne continued moving troops south. At the same time, General Horatio Gates led American troops to stop the British. In early October, the armies fought near Saratoga.

Burgoyne began the battle and tried to attack the Americans from behind. Benedict Arnold served under Gates and convinced Gates to send men to meet the British. The fighting was fierce. Neither side won a clear victory. The Americans had about 300 casualties. The British suffered about twice as many.

Burgoyne learned that British reinforcements were coming from New York City. The general waited. After several weeks, Burgoyne found out the new troops were not coming. So Burgoyne decided to fight right then.

On October 7, the British attacked a much larger American army. After the fighting ended, the British began to retreat to another fort closer to Saratoga. The Americans followed and surrounded the British. On October 17, 1777, more than 5,800 British, Hessian, and Native American troops surrendered. General John Burgoyne had lost 86 percent of the force that had left from Canada in the summer.

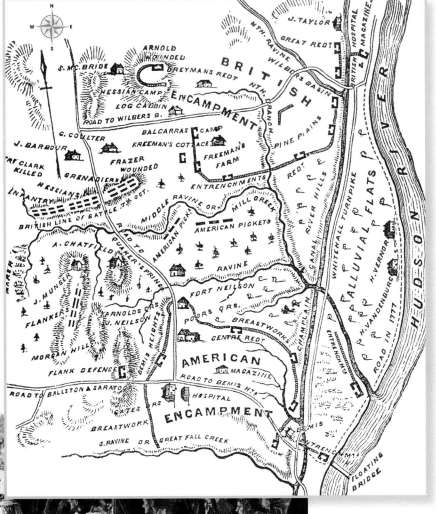

An Important Result

Historians say the Battle of Saratoga is one of the ten most important battles in world history. The reason is that Saratoga was the major turning point of the American Revolution. The British failed at dividing New England from the other states. Saratoga also had an important impact on American **diplomacy** (dih-PLOH-muh-see), or the effort between nations to keep good relations. France had been sending some aid to the Americans. After Saratoga, France felt sure Americans could win the war. So France decided to send troops to help the Patriots.

▲ Benedict Arnold played a key role in helping the Americans win at Saratoga. Later, though, he would turn against the Patriots to help the British as he conspired to turn his command of West Point over to them. In return, he received money and became a general in the British Army.

The New Year

Until the French arrived, the Continental Army would fight many battles during the spring of 1778.

The British decided to move troops from Philadelphia back to New York. The British wanted to leave the region before French ships reached Chesapeake Bay. On the retreat, the troops of Washington once again fought the British troops in New Jersey.

Monmouth Courthouse

On June 28, the Americans and British met near Monmouth Courthouse. American General Charles Lee managed the attack poorly. The Americans retreated, and Washington took command of the American forces. The entire American army moved up to face the British. The response was a **counterattack** (kown-ter-uh-TAK), or an action based on an earlier attack. The day was so hot that men died from the heat. The fighting went on for hours. Monmouth Courthouse became the longest nonstop battle of the Revolution.

✔

CHECKPOINT

Make Connections

Countries often rely on allies to help fight wars, as the Americans counted on the French. During the recent wars in Iraq and Afghanistan, which were some of the nations that aided the United States?

The fighting ended near sunset. The surviving soldiers on both sides were tired from the battle and the heat. In the evening, the British continued on to New York.

Although the Americans did not defeat the British, the Battle of Monmouth was important. Monmouth showed the courage and skill of George Washington on the battlefield. And both sides saw how well the Americans could fight after being trained at Valley Forge.

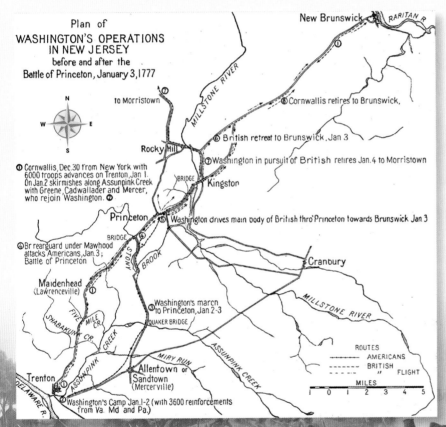

THEY MADE A DIFFERENCE

Mary Ludwig Hays (1754–1832)

During battle on hot days, women sometimes brought men pitchers of water to help keep them cool. These women were given the nickname "Molly Pitcher." One of these "Mollys" became famous for her action at Monmouth Courthouse. Mary Ludwig Hays was married to a member of George Washington's artillery forces. During the battle she was seen helping her husband load his cannon. Some stories say she fired the cannon herself after her husband was wounded. Hays later became known as the most famous "Molly Pitcher," though a woman named Margaret Corbin also fired a cannon during another battle.

A French officer fighting for the Americans praised George Washington for stopping the American retreat at Monmouth and preparing the army to fight again.

Monmouth marked the last major battle in the North between the Continental Army and the British.

Battles in the West

Some fighting during the Revolution took place outside the states in the north and east. The American forces tried to invade Canada. But the Americans had no success. Americans also fought in lands west of what is now Ohio. The British held several Ohio forts.

The British forts were in Illinois and Indiana. But the British also attacked settlers in what later became Kentucky. In 1778, Colonel George Rogers Clark proposed attacking British forts to the north. Clark led a small force west and sailed down the Ohio River. The Americans took Kaskaskia and Cahokia, in Illinois.

Vincennes

Soon the Americans controlled the British fort in Vincennes, in what is now Indiana. After the loss of Vincennes, the British took action. In December 1778, British soldiers joined with Indians. The two forces became **allies** (A-lize), or forces that fight on the same side. The two groups came from Detroit to attack the Americans left in Vincennes. The British easily took back the fort. British commander Henry Hamilton sent most of the men home for the winter. Hamilton planned to take back the other American forts in the spring.

Retaking Vincennes

Clark heard about the small British force guarding Fort Sackville at Vincennes. Clark decided to retake the fort before more British soldiers could arrive. So the American troops traveled across Illinois in February 1779, with about 170 men.

In Vincennes, Clark and his men tricked the British. The Americans flew many flags and fired rapidly at the fort. The British thought the Americans had a much larger force. The British fired back with artillery and muskets. But the Americans were well hidden. The British commander could not hold out against the Americans. So the British surrendered the fort to Clark.

PERSONAL PERSPECTIVE

George Rogers Clark described his thinking before his march on Vincennes:

"I am resolved to take advantage of his [Hamilton's] present situation and risk the whole [everything] on a single battle. . . . I know the case is desperate, but, Sir, we must either quit the country or attack Mr. Hamilton. No time is to be lost. . . . Great things have been affected by a few men well conducted. Perhaps we may be fortunate."

The event at Vincennes has been called one of the most heroic actions of the American Revolution. The victory established an American military presence in the West for the first time.

The Root of the Meaning

The word **artillery** is from the Old French *artillier,* "to provide with engines of war."

▼ While crossing Illinois, Clark and his men marched through rain and waded through ice-cold water several feet deep.

Native Americans in the Revolution

During the revolution, Native American tribes fought for each side. Most that chose to fight were allies of the British. The British intended to keep American settlers from taking land, including Native American land.

The Mohawks of New York were powerful allies for the British. The Mohawks were part of the Iroquois **Confederacy** (kun-FEH-duh-ruh-see). A confederacy is made up of groups that join together. The Iroquois Confederacy consisted of six tribes. Several Iroquois fought for the British. Two Iroquois tribes helped the Americans. In New England, Native Americans who had become Christians also supported the Patriots. Some volunteered to fight in early battles.

Native American Battles

In 1778, 500 Iroquois joined Loyalist troops and attacked American settlers and troops. Some of the worst fighting happened in western Pennsylvania. Hundreds of Patriot soldiers were killed and homes were burned.

Revenge

In 1779, an American force of about 4,000 gathered for revenge. The troops marched into Iroquois territory in New York. The Americans defeated the Iroquois and Loyalist forces on the battlefield. Native American farms and villages were destroyed.

PRIMARY SOURCE

American soldier William Barton kept a diary as he helped destroy Iroquois villages. Here is part of what he wrote:

"The whole army employed . . . in gathering the corn, and burning it in their huts, which were in number about eighty or a hundred, and much the largest quantity of corn I have yet seen in any one place since I have been out."

◀ The Iroquois who fought for the British were led by the Mohawk chief Thayendanegea. The British called him Joseph Brant.

Summing Up

- Washington's army won major victories at Trenton and Princeton, New Jersey, but lost at Brandywine and Germantown, Pennsylvania. For a time, the British held the American capital of Philadelphia. When they left in 1778, they fought the Americans at Monmouth Courthouse in New Jersey. The Americans did not win, but they demonstrated the improved training they had received during the winter at Valley Forge.

- During 1777–1778, the Americans won important battles in New York and in the West. The victory at Saratoga helped bring France into the war to aid the Americans. In Vincennes, George Rogers Clark made a daring attack on the British.

- Throughout the war, Native Americans helped both sides. Both Native Americans and settlers carried out raids that destroyed each other's towns.

Putting It All Together

Choose one of the following research activities. Work independently, in pairs, or in small groups. Share your responses with your class, and listen to others present their work.

1 France was not the only foreign country to aid the Americans. Research which other countries were American allies during the war. Then make a list or graph showing how each nation helped.

2 Benedict Arnold was both a brave general and a traitor. Learn more about his life. Write one paragraph exploring how he helped the American cause and another explaining how he hurt it. Then write about what happened to him after the war.

3 One of the most famous images of the Revolution is a painting of George Washington crossing the Delaware River in a small boat. Find this painting online and research whether or not it was an accurate view of what the crossing might have been like.

FEEDING THE TROOPS AT VALLEY FORGE

Cartoonist's Notebook by Denis O'Rourke and Heidi W.
Illustrated by Gary Freeman

IN THE WINTER OF 1777-1778, GENERAL WASHINGTON AND THE CONTINENTAL ARMY WERE ENCAMPED AT VALLEY FORGE, 32 KILOMETERS (20 MILES) FROM THE HEADQUARTERS OF THE BRITISH TROOPS IN PHILADELPHIA, PENNSYLVANIA.

CONTINENTAL ARMY SOLDIERS BUILT THEIR OWN CRUDE CABINS AND ENDURED BITTER COLD WITH WANING SUPPLIES. THEY WERE HUNGRY AND TIRED.

BRITISH SOLDIERS OCCUPIED HOMES AND BUSINESSES IN PHILADELPHIA AND WERE WELL FED.

GENERAL WASHINGTON, WE ARE DANGEROUSLY LOW ON FOOD. WHEN WILL WE RECEIVE MORE SUPPLIES?

I FEAR THE LOCAL FARMERS ARE HOARDING FOOD.

CAPTAIN ANDERSON, YOU MUST TAKE YOUR TROOPS TO SEEK FOOD AND SUPPLIES FROM FARMERS. SURELY GOOD PATRIOTS WILL SHARE THEIR LIVESTOCK WITH OUR SOLDIERS.

CAPTAIN ANDERSON'S TROOPS SOON COME ACROSS THE GREELEY FARM.

GOOD FARMER, THE CONTINENTAL ARMY NEEDS YOUR HELP.

BY THE ORDERS OF GENERAL WASHINGTON, I AM SEEKING SUPPLIES FOR THE CONTINENTAL ARMY. ARE YOU A PATRIOT? CAN I SECURE THREE QUARTERS OF YOUR LIVESTOCK AND GRAIN, SIR?

SIR, I AM A PATRIOT, BUT I CANNOT GIVE UP MY FOOD. IT MUST FEED MY FAMILY THROUGH THE WINTER.

SHOULD CAPTAIN ANDERSON TAKE THE LIVESTOCK AND GRAIN FROM FARMER GREELEY FOR WASHINGTON'S TROOPS OR NOT? EXPLAIN YOUR ANSWER AND SUPPORT YOUR CLAIMS.

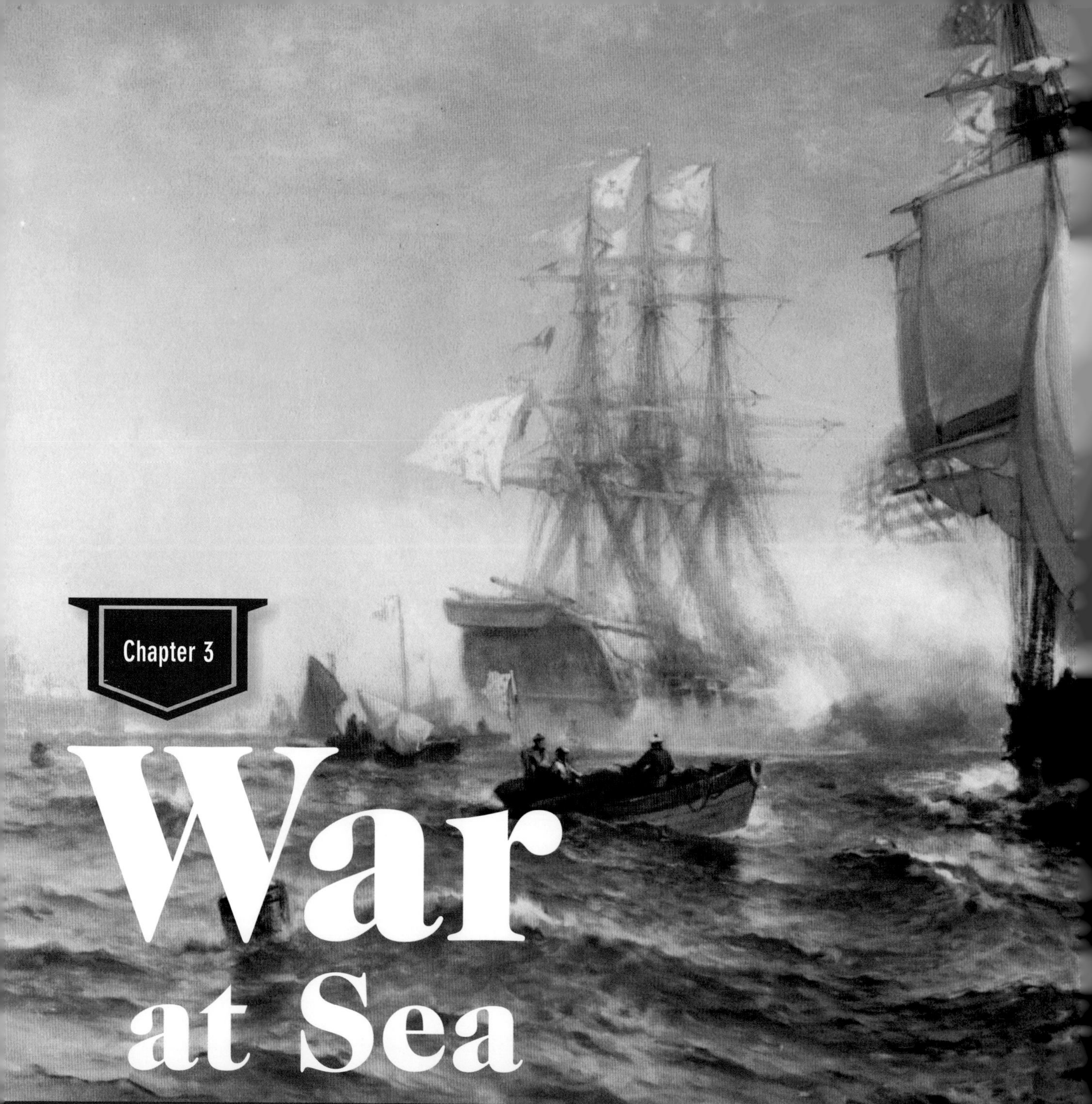

Chapter 3

War at Sea

What was the nature of naval warfare during the American Revolution?

ESSENTIAL VOCABULARY

- grenade page 34
- gunboat page 33
- navy page 31
- privateer page 32
- raid page 31
- traitor page 34

▲ British ships fired on several New England towns during the first months of the war. The firing set fire to Falmouth, Maine.

Armies on land fought most battles of the Revolution. But battleships at sea also played an important part in the war. When the war began, the colonists did not have a **navy** (NAY-vee)—the military force that fights at sea. In the fall of 1775, Congress asked that cannons be put on several ships. Congress also ordered the building of new ships. Great Britain already had a large navy. Many British war ships carried at least 60 cannons.

Early Battles

Early in the war, New Englanders sometimes fought the British at sea. In May 1775, the people of Machias, Maine, took over a British ship. The Patriots then captured a British warship. Citizens on the Massachusetts coast also battled British ships.

The early Continental navy carried out a **raid** (RADE), or sudden attack. The raid took place in the Bahamas, a British colony in the Caribbean Sea. Sailors attacked a fort and captured cannons and gunpowder.

Privateers

Some privately owned American ships attacked enemy ships. The American ships, called **privateers** (pry-vuh-TEERZ), received payment from the government. The privateers caused major damage to British ships. A privateer would try to capture a merchant ship with goods. The privateer owner would sell off all the goods. The sailors on the privateer would share the money. Privateer sailors often earned more than sailors in the Continental navy.

Privateers in Battle

Most privateers avoided fights with British warships. But one notable sea battle took place between the American privateer *Congress* and the British ship *Savage*. The ships met off the coast of Charleston, South Carolina, in 1781. The British captain did not know that the American ship carried large guns. In the battle, the *Congress* destroyed a large part of the enemy ship. The Americans forced the *Savage* to surrender.

Arnold's Fleet

Benedict Arnold built ships that sailed on Lake Champlain, a lake between New York and Vermont.

Late in 1775, Arnold led an invasion of Canada. Americans had learned that the British planned to attack American forces in northern New York. The British plan was to come from Canada across Lake Champlain. The job of Arnold was to stop the British.

Arnold called together skilled workers at the southern end of the lake. The workers repaired some small boats. The men also built new boats that Arnold had designed.

▼ **During the Battle of Valcour Island, Arnold lacked enough experienced sailors to fire the cannons. At times he had to aim them himself.**

Some of the armed boats, or **gunboats** (GUN-botes), used sails and oars. Other gunboats only used oars. All the gunboats carried small cannons. The wood used for the gunboats caused the ships to leak easily. Arnold was forced to use soldiers with no sailing experience. Arnold knew how to sail and trained the men. Then Arnold waited for the British to approach the small American fleet.

▼ This life-sized model of one of the boats Arnold used on Lake Champlain is kept at a museum in Vergennes, Vermont.

Valcour Island

The British had about twice as many ships on Lake Champlain as did the Americans. The British ships also had more powerful cannons. The two fleets met on October 11.

Arnold located the American ships between the mainland and Valcour Island so that the British could not see the fleet. The largest British ship could not get into position to attack. The smaller boats on each side blasted at each other. The fighting went on all afternoon. In the end, many American boats had been badly damaged.

The American boats slipped away in the dark of night. The next morning, the British began to chase the Americans down the lake. Another battle began. Arnold finally ordered the American sailors to go ashore. The Americans burned the ships. Then the men ran into the woods.

An Important Battle

The Patriots lost the Battle of Valcour Island, but the navy battle was important. The British had to build boats to sail on Lake Champlain, as did Arnold. The work delayed the British attack on Fort Ticonderoga. So the Americans had time to build up forces near Ticonderoga. As a result, the Americans were better prepared when General Burgoyne invaded New York the next year.

✔
CHECKPOINT

Reread

Look again at the actions Benedict Arnold took before and during the fighting at Valcour Island. What do you think was the most important decision he made? Why?

Another Naval Hero

Benedict Arnold acted as a Patriot before taking action to help the British. But Arnold did become a **traitor** (TRAY-ter)—a person who betrays his country. So John Paul Jones gets credit as the greatest American naval hero of the war.

In 1778, John Paul Jones sailed the *Ranger* across the Atlantic. The *Ranger* attacked British ships close to home. Jones also raided the English town of Whitehaven. Jones and his crew burned a ship there. As British ships made chase, Jones captured the British ship HMS *Drake* off the coast of Ireland.

The *Bonhomme Richard*

In 1779, Jones sailed from France in command of the *Bonhomme Richard*. On the ship, American sailors fought one of the most famous sea battles in American history. The *Bonhomme Richard*

▲ The *Bonhomme Richard* was an old merchant ship that had been equipped with forty cannons.

sailed with three other ships. The American ships came upon two British warships guarding merchant ships. The *Bonhomme Richard* took on the larger of the two British vessels, the *Serapis*.

Jones moved closer to the enemy, but the *Serapis* had more guns. The *Serapis* soon destroyed large parts of the American ship. The *Bonhomme Richard* began to sink. The British captain asked if Jones was ready to surrender. According to legend, Jones replied, "I have not yet begun to fight." The Americans fought off British sailors who tried to board the ship. Then a Patriot sailor threw a small bomb, called a **grenade** (greh-NADE), onto the *Serapis*. The explosion caused great damage and the British surrendered.

Summing Up

▶ The Americans had no navy at the start of the American Revolution, while the British had hundreds of naval ships. Americans in Machias, Maine, used a captured British merchant ship to win the first naval battle of the war. Privately owned ships called privateers helped the Americans capture hundreds of British merchant ships.

▶ On Lake Champlain, Benedict Arnold built a small fleet that fought a much larger and stronger British force. Arnold lost the Battle of Valcour Island, but his actions on the lake forced the British to delay a land attack in northern New York. That delay gave the Americans time to strengthen their forces in the region.

▶ John Paul Jones was one of the most illustrious heroes of the American Revolution. His greatest victory came in 1779 on the *Bonhomme Richard*. Jones refused to surrender even as his ship sank, and he managed to capture a more powerful British vessel.

Putting It All Together

Choose one of the following research activities. Work independently, in pairs, or in small groups. Share your responses with your class, and listen to others present their work.

1 The British used ships as prisons where they kept captured Americans. Go online to find a description of how the prisoners were treated on those ships.

2 What war technology at land and at sea was developed during the American Revolution? Make a poster or a digital presentation that explores this topic.

3 The colonies benefited from the French navy during the American Revolution. What role did the French navy play in the Battle of Yorktown, which ended the war.

Chapter 4

The Road to Final Victory

How did the Americans manage to turn the tide against the British and win their independence?

ESSENTIAL VOCABULARY

Because of the British siege, food was close to running out in Charleston when the Americans finally surrendered.

▲ Banastre Tarleton was just twenty-six years old when he was put in charge of a cavalry unit in the South.

The Siege of Charleston

Next, the British targeted Charleston, South Carolina. On ships, British forces arrived outside the city in February 1780. General Benjamin Lincoln commanded the Americans. Lincoln saw the British forces move into place and then tried to pull the American troops out of the city. But local officials convinced Lincoln to stay. Staying was an error. The British were able to surround Charleston and cut off routes in or out of the city. In May, Lincoln surrendered. By then, more than 5,000 Americans had been taken prisoner. Charleston was one of the worst Patriot defeats of the war.

After Charleston, the British continued to win in South Carolina. Success came from a British cavalry officer named Banastre Tarleton. Violent actions earned Tarleton the name of "Bloody" Tarleton. In North Carolina, American soldiers surrendered, but Tarleton let British troops bayonet some prisoners. In 1780, the **cavalry** (KA-vul-ree), or troops on horseback, for Tarleton defeated several thousand Patriots near Camden, South Carolina.

The last major land battles of the American Revolution took place in the South. At the end of 1778, the British **occupied** (AH-kyuh-pide), or took control of, Savannah, the capital of Georgia. Next, the British took over almost the entire state. Americans, with the help of French allies, tried to retake Savannah in October 1779. The attempt failed. The Americans and French suffered higher casualties than the British Army.

The Root of the Meaning

Charleston came from the name Charles Town. The city was named for Charles II of England, who had granted the charter to the English settlers of South Carolina during the 1660s.

Turning the Tide

The main British forces headed north. Local Loyalists helped along the way. Then Americans won a major victory at King's Mountain, South Carolina. The British suffered 400 casualties, while the Americans lost fewer than 100.

Marion's Raiders

More American success came in rural areas. General Francis Marion led small groups of soldiers on raids in the remote countryside, called **backcountry** (BAK-kun-tree). Outnumbered, the American troops attacked Loyalists and the British. Tarleton chased Marion for miles through a swamp. People began calling Marion "the Swamp Fox." The success of Marion raised the spirits of South Carolina Patriots.

The Battle of the Cowpens

Daniel Morgan also worked in the backcountry. Morgan led a small group of men in South Carolina. A British commander sent Tarleton after Morgan. At first, Morgan got away. But the forces of Tarleton and Morgan finally met in a cow pasture in January 1781. At the Battle of the Cowpens, the Americans were again outnumbered. But Morgan had a talent for getting a great effort out of the American soldiers.

Morgan set up three lines of men. In the first line were sharpshooters. The sharpshooters killed more than a quarter of the advancing British troops. Then the first line retreated to join the second line. New firing led to more British deaths. The cavalry also arrived to help. In the end the Americans won a major victory.

◀ Francis Marion had been in Charleston during the siege but managed to escape the city before the British took control.

✔ CHECKPOINT

Make Connections

The actions of Tarleton's men would be called a war crime if they took place today. Go online to learn about the role of the International Criminal Court in hearing cases today that involve these types of crimes.

The Final Key Battles

From South Carolina, the main fighting traveled north. General Nathanael Greene was the American commander in the South. As more militia came to help, Greene took direct control of a growing army that prepared to fight the British forces at Guilford Courthouse, North Carolina.

Guilford Courthouse

Greene decided to use a strategy similar to what Morgan used at Cowpens. Greene used three lines of soldiers. The forces at Guilford Courthouse were much larger, however. So the fighting went on for more than two hours. Sometimes small cannonballs, called **grapeshot** (GRAPE-shaht), cut down soldiers from both sides. As the battle ended, the Americans retreated. British General Cornwallis claimed a victory. However, Cornwallis had lost many men, including some important officers. The British then fled north to Virginia.

THEY MADE A DIFFERENCE

Nathanael Greene (1742–1786)

From Boston to Valley Forge to the Carolinas, George Washington counted on the skills of Nathanael Greene. Born in Rhode Island, Greene helped form a militia there even before the war began. He took part in the siege of Boston and fought at key battles in New Jersey and Pennsylvania. At Valley Forge, Greene was instrumental in improving the supply lines for soldiers. His most valuable service came during the Southern campaigns. Historians praise the way he used small forces to disrupt British operations. After the Revolution, Georgia gave Greene land to thank him for his efforts. This was a common reward for veterans, and Greene needed it because he had spent most of his own money supporting the Patriot cause.

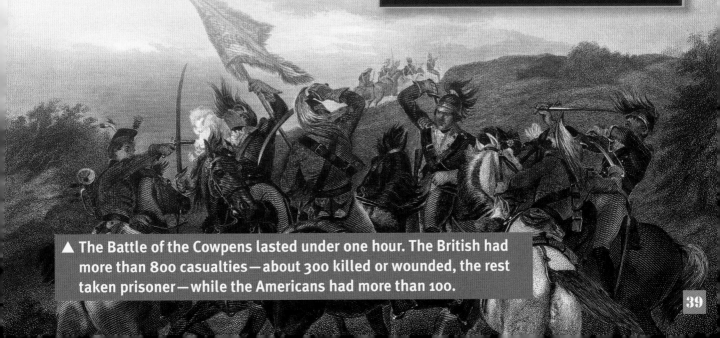

▲ The Battle of the Cowpens lasted under one hour. The British had more than 800 casualties—about 300 killed or wounded, the rest taken prisoner—while the Americans had more than 100.

Yorktown

By the fall of 1781, both sides had gathered large armies in Virginia. Cornwallis commanded an army at Yorktown, on the Virginia coast. George Washington wanted to attack the British in New York. Meanwhile, the French allies of Washington had sent a fleet of ships to Virginia. So American and French troops marched to Yorktown. The two armies and the French fleet combined and surrounded the British. Washington ordered a siege of Yorktown. In a few days, the Americans captured two British redoubts. Cornwallis had no choice. The British surrendered on October 19, 1781.

Yorktown was the last major victory of the war. After Yorktown, the British government granted independence to the colonies. Fighting still continued into 1782. In November, a small number of Americans fought British troops who were looking for supplies on James Island. Historians say James Island was the last battle in the American Revolution. On September 3, 1783, representatives of the American colonies, Great Britain, Spain, and France, signed the Treaty of Paris. The treaty officially ended the war.

▼ In 1780, Lord Cornwallis had just over 8,000 men to carry out his campaigns in the South. His officers often commanded Loyalist troops in battles against the Patriots.

PERSONAL PERSPECTIVE

James Thatcher was an American doctor at Yorktown. He described some of the action he saw during the battle:

"From the 10th to the 15th, a tremendous and incessant [non-stop] firing from the American and French batteries is kept up, and the enemy returns fire, but with little effect. . . . In the night they [cannonballs] appear like a fiery meteor with a blazing tail, most beautifully brilliant . . . descending to the spot where they are destined to execute their work of destruction."

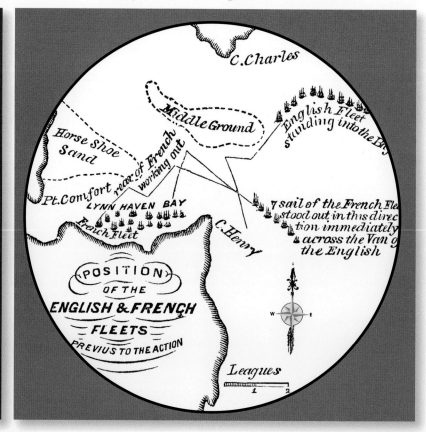

Summing Up

▸ Late in 1778, Great Britain began to fight in the South. It took control of two cities: Savannah, Georgia, and Charleston, South Carolina. The British also won an important victory at Camden, South Carolina. British victories made Loyalist militia eager to oppose Patriot forces.

▸ The Patriots fought back using small forces that attacked both British and Loyalist troops. Francis Marion and Daniel Morgan led some of these raids in the backcountry. Banastre Tarleton, a British cavalry officer, tried to stop both men, but failed. Morgan and his troops won a key battle against Tarleton at the Battle of the Cowpens in 1781.

▸ Much larger British and American forces met at Guilford Courthouse, North Carolina. The Americans were forced to retreat, but the British suffered high casualties. The battle there convinced the British to pull their main force out of the Carolinas and head for Virginia. The last major battle of the war took place there, at Yorktown. Washington's forces and French allies surrounded the British, who were forced to surrender. The American Revolution would soon be over, and the Patriots would have their independence.

Putting It All Together

Choose one of the following research activities. Work independently, in pairs, or in small groups. Share your responses with your class, and listen to others present their work.

1 Alexander Hamilton was one of the American artillery officers at Yorktown. Research his life and make a time line that shows some of the ways he helped the country during and after the Revolution.

2 Learn about the Treaty of Paris of 1783, which officially ended the American Revolution. What did the thirteen colonies gain besides freedom? List some of the terms of the treaty.

3 What happened to the American Loyalists after the Revolution? How were they treated by the Patriots after the war? Where did many of the Loyalists go after the war?

Victory and Independ

In 1775, American Patriots were not fighting a war for independence. The decision to seek a complete break from Great Britain came more than a year after the war started. From the beginning, however, Patriots fought to defend important rights. The rights included having local control and being represented in Parliament.

The Patriots faced many difficulties in the struggle for independence. The separate colonies now had to fight together. Also, not all Americans supported independence. Great Britain had one of the most powerful military forces in the world. But George Washington believed in the Continental Army. And Washington had a strategy for winning the war. The idea of American military leaders was to avoid fighting unless the chance of winning was good. American commanders also kept the forces moving. All the Americans had to do was survive until

ence

▲ George Washington enters New York after liberating the city from the British.

the British got tired of fighting so far from home. French aid also helped the American cause. And, as in any war, luck helped. In the end, after almost eight years of fighting, the Americans won independence.

The American Revolution ended in 1783, with the signing of the Treaty of Paris. On that day, the United States of America, a new independent nation founded on the principles of democratic freedom, was born. ▶

How to Write a Diary Entry

Historians use a variety of documents to learn about what happened in the past. Some of these are called primary sources. This means they were written by people who actually took part in events or watched them as they happened. One important type of source for understanding the American Revolution is the diary.

Many people first kept diaries to record their religious experiences. Others simply wanted to record what they did and felt from day to day. Some diarists hid their diaries so others could never read them. Others thought, or hoped, that one day someone would read these personal writings. Diaries often cover many years in a writer's life.

Presidents of the United States have kept diaries that give personal accounts of their years in office and the events of the time. Historians hope to learn from the "bird's-eye" or overall view of important events these diaries provide when they are made public.

Before starting a diary entry, you will need to decide what kind you want to write. Is it strictly for yourself? If so, then you can be as honest as you want in saying what you think about other people, or in describing your deepest feelings. But if you think you might show your diary to others, or that they might find it on their own, you should exercise more caution in what you write.

▼ This photo shows pages from one of George Washington's diaries. He kept diaries throughout almost his entire life.

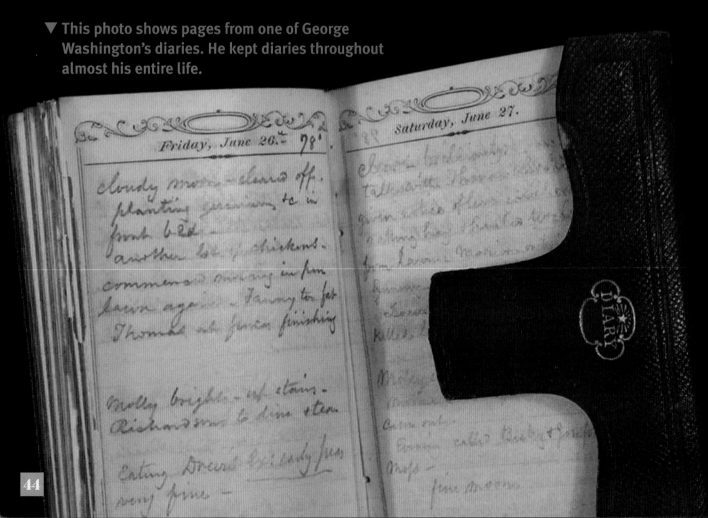

▲ If you write your diary by hand, using ink rather than pencil will make it easier to read as time passes.

A diary entry is written using the first person point of view, and it is usually written at the end of the day, every day. You should record the day's events while you can still remember them well. You might want to jot down notes during the day to help you remember important activities, or ideas you had. Writing the diary entry lets you say more about those thoughts and events than you put into your notes.

A typical diary entry has the day's date at the top. If you are traveling, you might also want to note where you are. Some diarists also describe the day's weather. Diaries can be handwritten in special books with blank pages. But you can also use regular pads or keep your diary on a computer.

At times, writers start the entry with "Dear Diary." This makes it seem as if they are writing a letter to someone. Pretending you have an audience who will read your words might help you pay attention to such things as spelling and grammar. The best diarists have great skill with words. They use details to explain their world as they experience it.

Try writing one diary entry. If you enjoy it, then try to keep writing every day. If you save your diary, one day a historian might find it. Your words could help others understand the life of a typical American student of the early twenty-first century.

Glossary

ally   (A-ly) *noun* a country or group that aids others during wartime (page 24)

artillery   (ar-TIH-ler-ee) *noun* large guns that are usually moved on wheels and require more than one person to load and fire (page 20)

backcountry   (BAK-kun-tree) *noun* a less settled area of land (page 38)

bayonet   (BAY-uh-net) *noun* a metal blade that attaches to the end of a gun (page 9)

boycott   (BOY-kaht) *noun* a refusal to interact with an individual or a group in order to protest conditions (page 8)

campaign   (kam-PANE) *noun* a series of battles fought in one region (page 12)

cavalry   (KA-vul-ree) *noun* soldiers who fight on horseback (page 37)

confederacy   (kun-FEH-duh-ruh-see) *noun* groups of people or nations joined together (page 26)

counterattack   (kown-ter-uh-TAK) *noun* the forward motion of one side in a battle after it is first attacked by the enemy (page 22)

diplomacy   (dih-PLOH-muh-see) *noun* the effort between nations to keep good relations and settle any problems peacefully (page 22)

frontier   (frun-TEER) *noun* the area beyond settled areas (page 7)

grapeshot   (GRAPE-shaht) *noun* tiny metal balls fired from a cannon at one time (page 39)

grenade   (greh-NADE) *noun* a small explosive, usually thrown (page 34)

gunboat   (GUN-bote) *noun* a small boat that carries several small cannons (page 33)

Hessian   (HEH-shun) *noun* a German soldier who fought for the British during the American Revolution and was often called a mercenary by Patriots (page 17)

line   (LINE) *noun* an arrangement of soldiers or military defenses (page 11)

Loyalist   (LOY-uh-list) *noun* a person who remained loyal to Great Britain during the American Revolution (page 7)

militia	(mih-LIH-shuh) *noun* a part-time army made up of the men of a town (page 8)
minuteman	(MIH-nut-man) *noun* a member of a militia in Massachusetts (page 9)
musket	(MUS-ket) *noun* a gun with a long barrel that is smooth on the inside (page 9)
navy	(NAY-vee) *noun* a country's military force specializing in battles at sea (page 31)
occupy	(AH-kyuh-py) *verb* to take over and hold by force (page 37)
Parliament	(PAR-lih-ment) *noun* the part of the British government that makes laws (page 7)
Patriot	(PAY-tree-ut) *noun* a colonist who opposed British laws and wanted to fight British troops (page 7)
privateer	(pry-vuh-TEER) *noun* a privately owned ship that receives permission from a government to attack enemy ships for financial gain (page 32)
raid	(RADE) *noun* a surprise attack on an enemy during a war (page 31)
redoubt	(rih-DAUT) *noun* a small fort that is built quickly, often out of dirt and rocks (page 11)
reinforcements	(ree-in-FORS-ments) *noun* soldiers and supplies sent to help an army during battle (page 20)
retreat	(rih-TREET) *verb* to pull back from the main fighting during a battle (page 9)
siege	(SEEJ) *noun* a military effort to surround a city and prevent the people inside from receiving food or supplies (page 12)
spy	(SPY) *noun* a person who secretly collects information about an enemy (page 17)
traitor	(TRAY-ter) *noun* someone who betrays a country, group, or person (page 34)

Index